Academe

SOUTH WEST: Lymington 73050

In memoriam
ARTHUR RAYMOND GROVES
1907–1973

Academe
Paul Groves

SEREN BOOKS
*1988

Seren Books is the book imprint of
Poetry Wales Press Ltd.,
56 Parcau Avenue, Bridgend, Mid Glamorgan

© Paul Groves, 1988

British Library Cataloguing in Publication Data

Groves, Paul
Academe.
I. Title
821'.914

ISBN 0-907476-98-8

All rights reserved. No part of this publication may be
reproduced, stored in a retrieval system, or transmitted in
any form or by any means, electronic, mechanical,
photocopying, recording or otherwise, without the
prior permission of the author.

Cover designed by Jeane Rees from an idea by Paul Groves
Cover photograph: at Kelmscott Manor,
Oxfordshire, by the author

Published with the financial support of the
Welsh Arts Council

Typeset in 10½ point Palatino
by Megaron, Cardiff
Printed by Antony Rowe Ltd., Chippenham

CONTENTS

7	All Hallows' Eve
8	Amends
10	Anagram Soup
12	Anniversary Soak
13	A Special Treat
15	At the Gentleman's Outfitter
16	Bluestocking
17	Children Playing
18	Coming in to Land, Nova Scotia
20	Cresting
22	Display
23	Emma
25	Entre Nous
26	Eric and Maiden
29	Fairies
30	Fall Guy
31	Forgetting Water
32	Gauging the Pneuma
34	Greta Garbo
36	Here
37	Heroine
38	Higginbotham Takes All
40	Hummingbird
41	*In Extremis*
43	Jim and Suzi Yo
44	Major Moore
45	Mrs Jekyll and Mrs Hyde
46	Nightfall
47	Nocturne
48	Obsequies
50	Parrots
51	Progress Report
52	Remembering

53	Sport
54	Stairs
56	Sun Poem
57	Tag
58	The Advent of Fatherhood
60	The Butt of all my Dreams
61	The Girls at St Catherine's
62	Turvy-Topsy
64	Twenty Minutes
65	Tyrell's Barn
66	Unacknowledged Legislator
68	Wanda at Dusk
69	Writing to Alison Myers

All Hallows' Eve

The heads of antelopes adorn the walls.
Their plastic eyes have witnessed savagery
as meals were disembowelled and wines decapitated
with the sound of buckshot. The captain
stalks these walks, a living ghost dedicated
to the butchery of flowers he crams in vases
adorned with sea-shells older than civilization.
His monocle steams up at the thought of squid
waiting for the sea-caves of his stomach,
Montrachet thick as blood, and pastries
aborted from the hands of the hirsute chef.
Guests will arrive soon, women with dresses
revealing a winkle navel, men who sell
armaments to developing Third World nations.
The servants are decked in the livery
of hand-picked angels from the castle's gardens:
their cheeks are from the orangery, and for eyes
lavender has been culled without superstition.
It promises to be a memorable ball; the speeches
will live on, trapped in the rafters' cobwebs
like beautiful flies, as the crab-like spiders move
delicately across their traceries of lace.

Amends

The talk with the solicitor reverses
into gibberish.
                He walks backwards
to the filing cabinet.
                        My wife speaks
while inhaling.
                  Traffic reverses down
the street outside.
                      Things gathering speed,
autumn phasing into summer, the sands filling
with families who eat picnics
dessert first.
                The plate her anger smashed
dances up onto the dresser, intact.
That clandestine affair yields
to an eminent foreclosure.
                          Happiness
burns the edges of the photograph.
                              Soon
all is engulfed in our younger selves'
smiles.
        Is this really a second chance?
                                The bells
cough recklessly in their spire; relatives
promenade like pre-war socialites in Baden-
Baden, covering where they have been
as if it is new ground.
                  The film sticks
at the kiss, that explosive moment
where the altar-rail glows like a nuclear
aftermath, and the organ locks
between gears.

Now we are in proper sync.
A revised future. Untried years ahead,
unsullied sheets, unblotted copybooks.
Yet again she reaches for that plate.

Anagram Soup

My sideburned uncle wears a caliper.
He raves and lurches, a Civil War replica,
ordering Southern Comfort, sitting on cane chairs
in the hotel conservatory, tapping saccharine
tablets into his coffee. *Once by canoe,
my boy, I crossed the raging ocean,
rounding Cape Horn
with no earthly chaperon.
Another time I used to breed carthorses;
trained them to the constancy of orchestras.
I stuffed one once for Drury Lane — on casters;*

*that was the year I had an affair with an actress.
We dined out regally: champagne and caviare.
Lesser sorts regarded us with avarice.
Her apartment was gilt-chandeliered, high-ceilinged.
I was her escort, suave and full of diligence.
When we split up, there wasn't much to celebrate.
I went to leasing large marquees, erectable
in a morning, for garden parties. It wasn't cheap,
and I made a fortune.* He polishes a peach,
and frowns. These days he reminisces with chesty
authority, scared of the figure with the scythe

and hour-glass. His gramophone plays choirs
and twenties jazz; he always has an orchis
nearby like a mute and trusty chum;
otherwise, he eats little, doesn't sleep much,
and only leaves the hotel when my Citroën
takes him for a ride. Then he's a noticer;
he looks for everything from tarts to clerics.
I drive his crustiness around in circles.
He seems content. *Life these days has no climaxes:
interpret that how you will* he loudly exclaims,
taking snuff as if it were cocaine.

He still dreams he is covering oceanic
distances, though champagne means cold tea
nowadays. Where that actress is located
no one knows. However, he continued
where others would have quietly died, unnoticed.
He has the stubborn buoyancy of cork
instead of the resigned indifference of rock
that sinks too soon into a world of corpses.
He fiercely guards his claim to the breathing process.
Too soon he will succumb to death's dark coteries,
the underworld, the weirdly esoteric.

Anniversary Soak

What kind of love is this when she
Lifts down the urn from its high place
And takes the top off gingerly
As if about to see his face,

And then rolls down her stockings as
She did that first night they were wed,
While he lay back there, bold as brass,
A bronzed young god upon the bed?

What sort of memory is kept
Alive as both the taps are turned?
That marriage day they never slept
But like two endless fuses burned.

She steps into the swirling heat,
Uncertain whether she should stoop
Or kneel; she looks down at her feet,
And tips the ashes in. The soup

That greyly laps her limbs is him,
The only man she ever craved,
The only one to keep her warm,
With whom alone she misbehaved.

A Special Treat

The names still make me shudder — Trecco Bay,
Sandy Bay and Rest Bay. Brash and bracing,
The wind and water walloped one with racing
Body-blows. The sea, gunmetal grey,
Allured uncertainly; one had to brave it.
An icy dash! That towel: I used to crave it
In seconds, skin the colour of dead fish,
Eyes red-rimmed, teeth mad castanets.
The tedious annual epic of our visits

Made the bathe obligatory. I wish
I could have seen some virtue in it all:
That crowded coach descending on Porthcawl.
But no; we ate the kitsch of candy floss
And fish and chips, anonymous in the crowd's
Wash along the Eastern Promenade's
Reach, like refugees whose only loss
Lay in finding pleasure unforthcoming
Finally. It always felt like slumming

Shuffling through the Coney Beach arcades.
Vast machines were having a good time,
Grunting, clanging. I could hear them chime
Like Satan's clocks. As busy as old maids
Knitting frenziedly, they gurgled and
Flashed, an electronic, seismic land
Of vapidness. Our precious pennies were
Too soon gobbled by these manic beasts.
Toffee apples loured. Gigantic fists

Whizzed past: seats, occupants in a blur
Of squealing squeamishness. Too quick! Too quick!
Sobriety was someone being sick
Against a fence. The deadline for departure
Loomed. The light was failing, and the waves
Were yet more hostile. As another heaves
And someone else crosses the car park for
A final leak, heads are counted and
The sliding door is mercifully slammed.

The nightmare was not over. Songs began,
Inexorably, cicadas in a dusk
Of tiredness and gritty socks. A flask
Was here unscrewed; there a cheap mouth-organ
Started its severe soliloquy
Always several seats too close to me.
This was the apogee of Sunday School,
A trophy for attendances maintained.
Masochism ruled. No one complained.

I hated it, but then I was a fool
Perhaps, for fellow fledgelings clearly loved
Being frozen, soaked, sandwiched and shoved
Around for umpteen hours. As the night
Wore on, exhausted youngsters dozed, or stared
At their reflection in the window, shared
By a relative. We tunnelled right
Through Glamorgan, numbed and drained and spent,
To dear forgiving mattresses in Gwent.

At the Gentleman's Outfitter

The draper drifts shiftily between
Victorian counters, past tie-racks
of potential nooses, boxes of folded
shirts which constitute the embryos
of business meetings, drawers of socks
like nylon balloons which feet
will inflate. Each day resembles
its predecessor and successor; there are
no surprises here. Time hammers itself
to the wall with regular old-fashioned ticks.
The board floor predates the *Lusitania*.
Fittings are contemporary with Oscar Wilde.
A window cleaner waves like a monkey
from his unreal vantage point; no chatter
is heard — just the quiet screech
of a chamois leather. Tea is taken
in a small cell next to the office.
Bags are lowered soundlessly into chubby
cups, scalded, and pressed gently by
silver teaspoons. Sugar falls in a little
gush, the hour-glass's last breath.
Mr Gittings has paced this fastness since
the year of the Coronation. He is always
immaculate. When he stands staring
into the depths of a daydream, you could swear
it is a mannequin with uncannily moist eyes.
The slightest movement shocks.

Bluestocking

Will you write that book on Annie
Besant from her acceptance of theosophy
Until her death in 1933?

You say you uphold her Fabian ideals.
You quote Ruskin: "Labour without joy is base".
Then someone comes to clean your place
For a pittance, while you have midday meals

And wine with liberated friends.
The char feather-dusts fine book-ends
In fashioned teak, and kneels and bends

With dustpan and brush. The joints you roll,
Odd silk stockings, feminist tracts:
All are tidied, the house made whole,
While you fulminate against the tracks

Society runs down out of control.
Could you salvage a nation's soul
While your daily fulfils her role?

Children Playing

They do not know it, but they are
dancing towards the edge of dance,
like a drunk cartoon mouse on a table.
Adulthood is waiting to swallow play,
digest it and defecate it to enrich the soil
of its own cramped gardens, with prams,
nappies, a sleeping greenhouse dreaming of stones.

They are reproducing the enemies of childhood:
mummies and daddies, the one ironing on a bank
of green, tidying cowslip cuffs, dandelion collars,
the other relaxing in an armchair of bracken,
sucking a pipe of grass, reading *The Air News*
easily in arms which will never tire of the pages.
The land reaches out to them, offers the sweets

of innocency, and the clouds are congenial gestures.
The brooks run clear with a told-you-so, told-you-so
babble over trinket stones. How strangely
the grey pastures of commitment and responsibility
allure; how much more driving to work magnetises
as myth than rolling over and over down
this rich hillside for ever.

Coming in to Land, Nova Scotia

The two-seater relaxes its grip
on the air; it is like dying
quietly in bed — until you see
the pain of fields blurring under you,
trees clenching their fists, rock outcrops
grazing like dinosaurs.
                      The engine
keeps you from that alien world —
but only just.
                It eases you into its
cold bath slowly; out there the wind
has something to say.
                      It knocks on your door
like a bellhop.
          You are your own
lift attendant; one slip, and it's
the basement, arms folded on chest.

Noise bounces off the land.
                    Birds scatter,
their primary purposes postponed, like gossips
called indoors to a steaming kettle.

A farm motors by at sixty; barns
show off their angles, Pythagorean showgirls.

Then the strip: finite, demanding discipline.

Eyes narrow.
           You are being swallowed up
by a countdown.
              The explosion
of wheels on grass!
                Horizons wobble;
the propeller dices up everything.
                              The sky is lifted
like a hatch.
        Stability
jerks you, breathless, into place.

A controlled cutout.
                The onrush
of silence.
      Past and future are slid apart,
twin doors, to reveal the hangar of now,
your monster insect trustworthy, obedient,
your body part of its brain.
                          The world
was never nicer.
                Compact.
                        Absolute.

Cresting

You undressed
where the heat was redefined
by the air conditioning. Silk.
We were drinking Algonquins. Fresh
pineapple juice. Meanwhile, Brisbane
was torturing barometers. The radio
spoke of storms heading our way.
We rooted through the electronic
twilight. Neon turned our room on
and off like a japer at the light-
switch. You sighed rhythmically,
the Coral Sea soughing and slavering
around the Reef. We had been up-
country on business. You were precise
and pinched, never taking off
your spectacles, forever quoting
your firm's options, or seeking
reassurances that our company would
deliver in good time. That meal
unwound you. Childhood appeared,
Mother playing the harmonium to
your delicate dancing, Father working
the forests, felling, processing. You told
how the jarrah trees were valued
for timber and oil, how your sister
lost an eye in an accident, and how
you mastered Poulenc on the flute.
I touched your breast this afternoon
like a teenager in the park. Red-
flowering gum and flame grevillea
egged me on. Waratah and wattle
orchestrated our desire. This is
a strange city, with its Windsor,
Ascot, Balmoral, names more familiar

than familiarity itself. The storm
is rolling in now, intense and theatrical,
the sky bruised and gasping, half
in pleasure, half in pain. Winds
burst through the oblique blinds.

Display

This greengrocer's is a psychiatric hospital.
We're all mad. Boredom and fear
account for tomatoes and potatoes equally.
When we're safe we're bored; when we're unsafe
it's because we are about to be eaten.
Whole kilos of us sit around dreaming
of teeth. And not just teeth: they are
mere gateways to the awfulness of digestive
juices, the unspeakable ignominy of bowels.
There is no treatment. The cabbages
do not get electroconvulsive therapy; the courgettes
are not taken for a walk in the sunshine.
It's static. Overcrowded. Desperate.
The feeling of doom is all-pervading. Despite
assertions to the contrary, citing
seeds of intelligence, the growth of awareness,
the fact remains: we are all vegetables.
Only on the other counter can one claim
colourful fruitiness, a Mardi Gras appeal:
oranges in tutus, lemons dancing the conga.
Here we are heavy and agricultural.
We have Iron Curtain faces. We are
committed to doubt, inaction, betrayal.
Although we are washed, we still feel dirty.

Emma

The school library tells me Freyssinet is to blame.
Pre-stressed concrete. His invention.
The school library tells me Arnold tried
to improve English secondary education
in the 1860s. The outcome seems to be
we have a school library in pre-stressed concrete.
Daily I come here, pre-stressed, a sixth former allowed
periods of silent study: no more serried ranks
of desks, the teacher a pneumatic drill
boring into the pavement thought wants to walk down.
"George Wickham is an unprincipled adventurer. Discuss."
A Mars bar and pocket fluff
are my dowry. That really is nicotine
on my fingers. The school library tells me
Jacques Nicot is to blame: another Frenchman.
Did Arnold take to tobacco on the Continent?
The incinerators have been vandalised
in the girls' toilets. The caretaker tells me
the place is autumnal with russet Lillets.
The school library tells me Jane Austen's cart
is preserved in Chawton bakehouse.
I notice how freshly menstrual is
the Hampshire brick. My parents were out when she
came round to listen to My Fabulous Records.
We sat in my room. On the bed. And we never
touched. It was electrifying; the air was blue
with static. My heart was doing the cross-country.
She sat with secretarial poise. Heavy metal.
That book says *Inside Comprehensive Schools, HMSO, 1970.*
It has concrete covers.

In forty minutes it will be lunch.
Tortured swede, floppy pork, hard-boiled eggs.
"An egg boiled very soft is not unwholesome,"
said Mr Woodhouse, the School Catering Manager,
when she went Uck! yesterday.
She sat with me at the smeared vinyl: "Can I
sample your newer acquisitions tonight?"
That sounded a bit posh. I bet she passes
and swans off to Bath University. Jane Austen fainted
when faced with the prospect of Bath.
"Her irony is primarily a matter of comprehension. Elaborate."
Last night I ached with desire.
Nothing venereal. My soul was enflamed.
Iron Maiden sounded somehow a distraction. She's doing
A level physics, getting her rocks off
to Newton's Law of Cooling. I bet she knows
that osmium is the heaviest metal, used,
inter alia, to make pen nibs. "Jane Austen used
a quill dipped in vitriol. Give examples."
This morning I dropped my pyjama bottoms
and looked at it. Perpendicular, precise and taciturn,
it reared from the very same coverlet where,
eight hours before, *she* had sat.
I think I'll have the faggots and peas
or the toad-in-the-hole, followed by spotted dick.
Still thirty minutes to go.
Such impotency! Such temptation!
I reach down covertly
under this library table, my face displaying
admirable sang-froid, and with febrile fingers
undress my Mars bar.

Entre Nous

"Keep it under your hat," we said.
"You can rely on me," she said,
and left it at that. More private than secret
was our tryst of words, more confidential
than private. "Don't worry, I shan't
tell a soul." We believed her. ("Except
my husband" she meant.) "That's fine
by me," he would have asserted. "Steve won't divulge
our neighbours' business. He's my best friend;
and what are best friends for, if not to be
repositories of one's trust?" We hardly knew
him, or Angela — the next domino, or
her sister. Soon the entire village smiled.
The postman whispered to the shopkeeper
who spoke with exaggerated softness to the vet.
The farm manager, everyone in the almshouses,
most of the primary school were *au fait*
within a week. This part of the county
will light up next, our names upon its lips,
gossip reddening cheeks and moistening eyes,
raising hands to speak behind, covertly.
Eventually the nation, Europe, the world
will be party to our personal affairs;
but we can derive satisfaction from the fact
that humanity will not tell anyone.
It will sensibly keep the matter to itself.

Eric and Maiden

WILL GIRL TRAVELLING on 12.30
Paddington-West Country Wed. Aug. 8
and reading *Poetry Review* please contact
Eric (fellow traveller with whom she
discussed poetry as far as Taunton).
Box number SA7

A whistle. The slam of a door.
Passengers shuffling through
with heavy cases. Platforms on either side
of an earthbound, wingless plane.

Movement, smooth as cream poured
into coffee. Settle back. Watch faces
flit away, as if you could shoot any
without it making much difference.

Sky. Dormer windows. Cars at a traffic
light. A landmark four miles off. A headquarters.
An expensive jet stacking for Heathrow.
More light. Look at your fellow travellers.

Old, reading a Mills and Boon. A child
with glazed eyes, expecting to be bored;
its no-nonsense mum unwrapping a sweet.
And someone reading *Poetry Review*. Dear God.

Eric's palms moisten. She is beautiful
and has a mind. She is all faculties
and loose-leaf files, Shakespeare
and Thom Gunn. Has to be.

"Er, I'm Eric..." It took an age to say.
It took Reading to say. "And I like poetry too.
Look. I have the same magazine,
the same issue." "Let's discuss poetry,"

she says. "Who knows: perhaps to Taunton."
Dear God. "Page 32?" "Page 32."
That invisible medium called
The Same Wavelength stretches between them.

By Newbury, it's the heavy petting of Rilke,
the heavy breathing of Schiller, the name-dropping
of Walt Whitman and Ivor Cutler.
Their polymathy knows no bounds.

The Vale of Pewsey glides past
in iambic pentameter. High clouds allow
azure caesuras to punctuate their being.
They zip through Wiltshire, and summer explodes

like Emily Dickinson smoking
a trick cigar. Hey, Eric — cut
the Group chat, and ask her name.
But all he says is Philip Hobsbaum.

Eric, who is she? Find out before
it's too late. The fool. He's even asking her
to spell Medbh McGuckian. Already
the rest of the carriage has ceased to exist.

Taunton falls like a guillotine.
It is mid-afternoon, and the race is run.
Lifetimes have been lived, continents traversed
in their honest talk, their soul-baring.

She gets up. She shakes his hand.
What does he say? He is flustered and proud
equally. The gods dictate he must stay on board.
He curses Exeter.

She gathers speed on the moving platform
and is plucked from sight. He settles back
with a suddenly jejune copy of *Poetry Review*
and eyes the space she occupied.

Fairies

Who are they for: themselves,
Us, nobody? Why inhabit
The interstices of our world, no longer
Countrified by bluebell and rabbit
But urbanized by concrete? Look, stranger,
On this island now: do you see elves

Or Cola cans along verges?
Romanticism is buried
With the Victorians. The Great
War banished goblins' unhurried
Domain of thistle, nut and lily-plate;
Perhaps deep primordial urges

Fleshed out as imps and nymphs may reappear.
I doubt it.
Computer games have little people which
Answer to our whims. No flit
Of lacy wing hovering over a ditch
Was so amenable. One could not steer

Lords of the undergrowth by simple handles.
Their logic was beyond
Our circuitry. Their very ease unsettled:
Lolling at sunset by some sylvan pond,
Sliding down toadstools, hiding in nettled
Banks lit by glow-worm candles.

If they ever existed where are they now?
What do they think of our economic
Realities, our materialism?
Their answers as usual are fey and gnomic.
They are more interested in a raindrop's prism,
Milking a hedgehog-cow.

Fall Guy

The hang-glider pilot is Icarus.
                                        He has taken off
inhibitions; he leaves them behind
like a shadow which shrinks in seconds,
the wind his master, the sun
his lodestone.
                As to the sky, there is
an inexhaustible supply.
                        Birds steer clear
of this man-hawk.
                  He has the show
to himself, the pretence of permanence,
the apeing of real power.
                    But apes
never discovered the wheel; and man
has yet to discover real flight.
                          Teleportation.
To Sydney in ten seconds, the mind
in overdrive, distance diminished to a countdown.
Here progress is staid, almost old-fashioned.
He is a pioneer, not exactly a balloonist
with vintage port and eyeglass, Shakespeare's plays
and anemometer, but a canvas
entrepreneur, a nylon Blondin
walking the firmament without a tightrope,
swimming without water, telescoping
acres of scarp and lowland with the instrument
of his own body.
                Pen-y-Fan recedes
as quickly as he advances.
                        He can hardly breathe
there is so much air.
                    How can he know
he will land on four bearers' shoulders?

Forgetting Water

It took a lifetime to remember it,
to avoid it when something chucked it
out of the skies, or when it lay around
in ambushing puddles. It took a lifetime
to clean your teeth with it. And then,
Father, I saw you relinquish the concept
of water. You jettisoned it with so
much else: furniture, religious beliefs,
the facts of life. You died like a man
who had nothing, a deposed emperor,
some desperate hobo slumped on a park bench,
a bishop who is longing to hear angels
but senses only his housekeeper's unhelpful cough.
You were spared most ironies and paradoxes:
you died simply, like a fire deprived
of anything to feed on. You took with you
what you thought of me, what you remembered
of our years together. No wonder people drink
to excess, adulterize, drive recklessly.

Gauging the Pneuma

A Swedish doctor, checking patients before and after death, has calculated that a human soul weighs 21 g.

It is such a little matter set against
the complexities of the day. Even expiry
can become routine. Relatives' grief
is relative. There are few absolutes;
though the ling is again triumphant among
the smooth rocks beside Lake Vättern.
When dead it lives as peat, animation
less useful than inanimation.
Dr Almqvist loves paradox.
It is as pleasing as the gentle whortleberry
which gives itself, like Christ, for
the greater good. Ten patients this month,
fifteen last, before that eleven.... The conclusions
are becoming inescapable. Averages bang
like an unfastened barn door. His youth
was spent pitchforking hay, collecting eggs,
milking goats. He does not believe
souls are pitchforked into Hell,
that eggs symbolise rebirth — even at Easter,
or that the Devil walks with cloven hoof.
These measurements tell all. The ECG monitor
sits uncomplainingly, a small god.
It speaks day and night. When the blips
phase into a monotonal plateau, quietus
has been reached. Disconnect the oxygen.
Forget the programmed impulse generator.
There are weightier matters on his mind.
Nurse Bengtsson is summoned. She comes quietly,
high cheekbones betraying Lapp ancestry,
her cool manner redolent of northern winters
so long as to pitch the world into coma.

Calibration and calculation are undertaken
with a minimum of fuss. The warm meat
is still respected. It has secrets to yield.
"Much as I suspected," he sighs
with gratitude. The exceptions are getting
to prove the rule. He removes his spectacles, and sees
Nobel judges convening approvingly.
This Almqvist . . . Really quite remarkable. . . .
Nurse Bengtsson checks his figures with a nod.
He checks her figure thoughtfully, then returns
to the cadaver, the chrysalis
from which the psychic butterfly has flown,
and recalls that "chrysalis" is from the Greek for "gold",
gramme after gramme after gramme.

Greta Garbo

A Japanese paparazzo photographer has been waiting outside her apartment for more than three years, but has never succeeded in getting a full-face picture

Mostly you get the din of the Franklin D. Roosevelt Drive,
traffic plying this throughway beside
the East River. Mostly you get the sense
of being alive, of being five time zones from home,
from that family rooftree in Kawasaki, one block
from the Sojiji Temple. I have captured
kids playing pat-ball at one two-fiftieth of a second
at f4, leaves drifting to the ground on East 52nd
at proportions of that speed, but
Dame Fortune stays elusive. For thirty eight months
she has not bought zucchini. I find this remarkable.
The Americans call a swede a rutabaga;
I call this Swede the whole vocabulary,
depending on my mood: witch, goddess, foil, mantrap.
It is as if she never lived, and all I have done
for a slice of my life is kick cans,
light up another Lucky Strike, hope yet again
to strike lucky. I suppose this is an odyssey
in pursuit of elusiveness itself, a quest
for the resurrection of beauty: Odysseus
blew a decade on his errand. There's time yet.
When the wind blows, desperate, down from Maine,
and it's thirty below, I curse and stamp
and spend all day in the diner, wiping
condensation from the pane, focusing.
He brings me soup, and tuts, scratching his head.
"I thought Polacks were the limit, but
you're something else." Life has become
a philosophical acceptance of loss, a conflation
of zilch and Zen. Something stirs,

but it is only the janitor humping garbage
onto the sidewalk for the next collection.
She made a movie called 'Joyless Street'
in 1925, the year my mother was born
high in the hills near Kawakami
where the snowflakes are huge, and the air silent.

Here

This was their home; now
It's ours. I can legally stop
Her taking a bath, him
Tapping pipe-ash into the cup
On the chair arm.
This is the house I plough

My future in, my field.
They have no more claim, yet
One month ago every brick was
Owned by them. I cannot forget
How she tripped up these stairs,
How they made love, here, where I yield

To sleep's allure tonight.
It is all silence. Time's
Mysterious agency somehow
Has split us like a log. Crimes
Are avoided thus. Trespass cannot show
Itself. The transaction is watertight.

Heroine

She used to flash her fingers through the flame
Of her lighter. "Nothing to it."
She beckoned me to take part in her game.
I could not do it.
"Poltroonery!" (Where did she get that word?)
Beside her, my reserve was reprehensible.
She had a way of making the absurd

Appear supremely sensible.
Appearances were all. With sleight-of-hand
She waived responsibility, forsook
Caution, and inhabited a land
Within which my inhibited self shook
With genuine trepidation. She would sit,
Legs dangling, at a third-floor window, or

Balance on the handlebars with quite
Amazing calm while gathering speed, sure
That each calamity would pass her by.
We were college colleagues, yet I learned
Whereas she taught. The years mysteriously
Had gained her a maturity I yearned
To equal. Whence did she derive immunity?

How were so many safety measures spurned
With such alacrity, with such impunity?
She preached free love, and got her fingers burned
At last. The last I saw of her she had
Bowed like a branch beneath the weight of snow,
Mainlining, gaunt, pre-eminently sad.
I didn't know what to say, and still don't know.

Higginbotham Takes All

A basket of fruit, a caddy of tea,
A set of brushes, a British sherry,
Two dozen eggs, a theatre ticket,
A long-playing record, a car-shine kit:
These were the prizes. The Village Hall
Hushed for the draw. An uneasy pall

Of silence settled over the crowd.
Colonel Leander ruffled the shroud
By picking the first name out of the hat.
"R. Higginbotham. A basket of fruit."
The applause was modest. He rose to be given
What the vicar's wife offered, like something from Heaven.

"Prize number two: a caddy of tea.
R. Higginbotham again!" Again he
Rose to his feet, and walked to receive it.
He bowed to the stage, and proceeded to leave it.
He sat, and he sighed, and he smiled. "The next
Is a set of brushes. Do I detect

A feeling that hat tricks are in the offing?"
The Colonel said. There was laughing and coughing.
His grin turned into a frown as he read
"R. Higginbotham". "Never!" one said.
"Fix!" yelled another. "They're all his," a third
Shouted. The vicar said, "Quite absurd."

They sifted the counterfoils; many names lay
Inside the hat. It was all fair play.
Higginbotham received the brushes,
And gave, in return, a set of blushes.
He returned to his seat, no longer merry,
Only to come by a bottle of sherry.

He won the eggs, and he won the ticket.
He won the record. The mood was wicked.
He was hissed and booed, and somebody shoved him.
Nobody present remotely loved him.
They hated his luck and him, and it
Was murder accepting the car-shine kit.

His was the sorrow and never the pride.
"You wait till I get you alone outside,"
Snarled an onlooker, albeit a crackpot.
"You jammy bastard, to win the jackpot."
Seething envy pervaded the hall
When Reginald Higginbotham took all.

Hummingbird

The hummingbird refuels
in mid-air from the hub
of a fuchsia flower.
Its belly is feathered white
as rapids; its eye
is smaller than a drop of tar.
A bodied moth, it beats
stopwatches into lethargy
with its wingstrokes.
Food it needs every fifteen
minutes. It has the metabolism
of a steam engine.
Its tiny claws are slight
as pared fingernail;
you could slip it with ease
into a breast pocket.
There it might lie, cowed
— or give you a second heart.

In Extremis

Librarians are at the bottom of the stress league
        (Manchester University research finding)

You feel you can bear it no longer.
Breaking point. A sunbeam
gatecrashes. Dervishes of dust dance
menacingly in its radiation. A leaflet
drifts ominously to the floor.
                      Outside
the sky dims. There could be a jumble sale
in the offing; perhaps a traffic warden will appear
or a restaurateur take a sign in
from beside his bay window.
These things do happen. You have to be awake
to the dark music of the universe, the way
a horse swishes its tail, or a fly lands
on a bacon sandwich.
                Books conspire
silently. Their words are imprisoned thoughts,
a Munch painting screaming mutely.
God, someone could be clipping their nails
this very second two streets away. A bulb
could capitulate, plunging a pantry into gloom.

And all the time literariness magnetizes
human filings. You stamp their passports
as they enter the country of their choice:
novel exercises or documentary diversions.
An immigrant with a moustache asks to use
the photocopier. There is danger here. You start
to perspire, but cannot bring yourself
to wind open the window. He thanks you
with savage civility. You smile desperately.

And will this ever end?
                    At seven
the door will slam with manic finality
and you will traipse out, smashed by the breeze,
stifling a malevolent yawn. A monstrous bus
will take you to your semi, sequestered
behind minefields of privet. There you will lie
in a hot bath, a decomposing sugar cube,
surfacing occasionally through a cloudbank of suds,
humming some irredeemable melody like a condemned man.

Jim and Suzi Yo

There is something wonderful about being eighteen.
Jim sits in the youth hostel refectory
playing patience. The lights are too bright,
the table-top too challengingly plastic.
He has walked a score of miles today, and his socks
glow quietly on aching feet. An Oriental comes in
fixing her hair. Her eyes smile
while her lips purse. Jim considers this to be
plainly inscrutable. Somehow they get talking.

Already it is ten o'clock. Two hours have flown
on gauzy wings. Suzi Yo can only say
Cheam, and *sausages*, and *Bide awee*
with any assurance. Otherwise, she stumbles
and blushes, suddenly beautiful as a water-lily
Jim thinks. He beams proudly, now able to say
nerihamigaki (toothbrush) and *hai okutan*
(four star petrol) and *nishikaze* (west wind).

Tomorrow it will rain. As he tramps
over Kinder Scout he will remember
plucky little Suzi Yo, grappling with English,
five feet two in her stockinged feet, and smile.
Henceforth, Edale and she will seem inseparable.
That evening together will haunt his future years.
As he eases down the grassy gradient
of middle age, he will recall her halting speech,
her dainty innocence, so like a rare butterfly.
He might even buy a Japanese car.

Major Moore

When Father died we had to fill the gulf.
Enter Major Moore. Would he be a bridge
over the abyss, or mere rubble tipped
into its depths? Already he was growing
an arm along Mother's shoulder, a solicitous
trailer to the main event of his wooing.

Beryl had been the tops. None could replace her;
but Mother was a suitable substitute
perhaps. I watched them in the park,
the Major twirling the ends of his egotism
as if it were a moustache, the lady
demure again, daft as a virgin in his clutches.

I counselled against him, mainly on intuition.
She was already besotted enough to say "Nonsense".
Had she mentioned her bank account? Did he know
those antiques were worth a cruise to the Bahamas?
Without a word being said, he started to ignore me,
a subaltern, a son of little standing.

When he suggested that long weekend in Brighton
all I saw were traffic lights at red,
warning gestures everywhere. He whipped
the ingredients for a mousse with new authority
in the widow's kitchen. My eye was wary still.
I watched his Scimitar grow diminutive,

the battle lost, and Mother in a haze
of sugary delights. I stood in the drive
like an orphan. The Army had won
without one drop of blood being spilt.
I wandered indoors and poured a dry vermouth.
Put on 'The Funeral March'. Sat and listened.

Mrs Jekyll and Mrs Hyde

My wife has been seeing another man.
He is the other side of me.
I'm beside myself with jealousy, and plan
Suicide to be finally free

Of this interloper. Contrariwise,
I am the lover, not the spouse,
Who runs hot fingers along her thighs
While he is somewhere out of the house.

Envy is reaching a fever pitch.
A showdown is due, and the cards speak blood.
My trigger finger begins to itch
As one or other of us gets in the mood

Which will clinch the deal: the other face down
Among the gnomes in the rockery.
My wife has been seeing another man,
And that other man is me.

Nightfall

Ruskin's seat at Brantwood, that slate throne
under the fretful shade of trees too attuned
to gossip and variance: where better to spend
one's last days than here, echoes of voices
among the leaves.
     And then that waterfall. . . .

Hour after hour he watched it, refusing
to stop.
     It flowed inside his veins.

Did he hear the laughter of Euphemia
before her affair with Millais?
     Did he hear
the possibility of faithfulness, or the reckless
welter of passion crashing over rock?

At the lip of the lake his *Jumping Jenny* lay.

Better to put your trust in a boat
with a woman's name than in a woman.

Was this really madness, after so much
brilliance, the shadow cast by too active and
too true a mind, as shadows encroached
on his grey, withered face?
     There must be
more to greatness than its dereliction.

There must be more to waterfalls
than their ability to yell at the moon.

Nocturne

(for Cal Clothier)

During the great drought of 1979
the women of Uttar Pradesh tilled
the fields at night in the nude,
believing this might please the god of rains

Arms silvered by moonlight; shoulders;
breasts imperfectly seen, then seen
perfectly, as a voyeur moon
scuds between clouds that bring no rain

yet. The god of heavenly water waits.
His eyes are full of women silently toiling
with nothing between their secret places and him.
He is touched by their nakedness,

by their faith in his good offices.
He will repay them, but not yet.
This is too good to miss, these beautiful bodies
in the ghostly fields, their men elsewhere, abed,

squalid in huts, worn by grief and effort
into early senility and some disease.
These are mere girls, the best of them, touched
lightly by the hand of adolescence.

Though boys from other villages will come
to claim their bodies, there is a pact
tonight between these soundless, uncomplaining
shapes at work and this dark god,

who relishes so much, and gives so much
when he does give. Too often he is lazy
or apathetic. He can be a tyrant;
mostly he sits and empties a dry hand.

Obsequies

The day she died they wept.
It was September, mellow
And mild. The morning crept
About on slippered feet.
The hush in the bordello
Was tragic, and the sweet

Stillness of the room
Was what she would have wished.
Pale ladies entered, came
To where her face lay, washed
And perfumed on the pillow,
And dwelt in silence. Yellow

Had been her colour, and
Flowers of that hue
Were round the bed; a stand
Of yellow roses stood
Beside the door, and through
It filed the neighbourhood.

The police chief came, and dabbed
His forehead, for the heat
And lifeless presence robbed
Him of his usual state
Of balance. This was other.
He knelt and kissed his mother,

And left the way he came.
A certain cabinet minister
Entered, breathed her name
Respectfully enough,
And registered with sinister
Glee the bit of stuff

He saw on Wednesdays. So
All paid their last respects,
Sorry to see her go,
A champion of her sex,
Of Fifi, Mimi, Lola. . . .
They laid her close to Zola

In Montmartre Cemetery
On Friday of that week
At twenty five to three,
Most regally entombed.
Each doxy dried her cheek,
And business was resumed.

Parrots

The parrot is sure of something. He has
a copywriter's tie for a body. He holds
his own at parties, high in the trees,
impressing all the flappers. His whole family
are show-offs; they tend to get
above themselves, preening in the lianas,
bowling through hot mist like an extrovert
leaving a Turkish bath. I envy
their composure, the way they turn
jungles into tunnels of love, the way
they fuss and prance like a child storming
a gem-box. All are egregiously overdressed:
pantomime dames one minute, foppish gallery
directors the next. And what have they
to be proud of? A voice like a chain saw,
gaudy sequin eyes, a bill as bent
as the delivery of a leg-spinner.
As for their haunts, these are venomous,
sweaty, vertiginous, decidedly seedy.
And yet, given the dourness of sloths,
the stolidness of capybaras, it is refreshing
to consider the existence of parrots, even if,
occasionally, they become one cocktail too many.

Progress Report

They say she was a dancer. The light
slams into her as the sun pushes
past a cloud. Her shadow is flattened
against the wall. They say she was
beautiful, though it is not on file, merely
lost among her boxes of photographs. The end
of the hospital corridor gets no nearer.
Doctor Shah passes at great speed, feet
blurred, stethoscope wild from his neck.
Birds beyond the glass fly at approximately
two hundred miles an hour. When she drops
her spectacle case, it races forlornly
towards the linoleum. Everything is propelled
more than she. Paso doble, foxtrot,
tango: that these limbs ever did those steps
seems impossible. This then is the meaning
of one's dotage. Senile dementia, dribbling,
forgetfulness, the picking up of a spectacle case
with glacial dynamism. Dust dances
in the afternoon beams. Leaves cavort
outside in a sudden eddy. She is uncertain
as to why she is edging down this corridor.
No Paul Jones. No black bottom. Just
this *danse macabre*. Soft-shoe shuffle.

Remembering

The farmyard is a set of duns
And ochres, a stagy Wyandotte wandering
Aimlessly into focus. More hens
Inspect minutiae at a distance, wondering
With tilted head and bald eye.
A tractor rusts

Into its own autumn of foxy
Inconsequence. Chaff rests
On a sill here, the rim of a water-
Barrel there. A collie scratches in
Distracted silence in a far quarter
Of this sunny calm. The barn

Is a hollow mountain, a cathedral
With hay instead of holiness stacked inside.
Stroll past that massive door, steal
A glimpse into gloom, where the wide
Sweep of a swallow's flight alights
On a high rafter. Is this the same

Boy with ruddy cheeks and summer shorts
Who, thirty Junes ago, dreamily came
Into his uncle's barn, carrying a pail,
To search among the straw for precious eggs,
And saw a letter resting on a bale,
And was tapped gently by a pair of legs?

Sport

I could not tell why the men used to go
badger baiting, with dogs, iron bars,
torches.
    I would see them trudging out
brazenly at dusk towards the forest, laughing,
whistling, the sun setting on their backs like
a bloodstain.
    All I know about badgers is
that they are nocturnal, secretive, clean,
bedding their setts with grass and bluebells,
digging ordure pits some way from their homes.
Digging would take place under a full moon,
spades flashing eerily between the trees, guards
watching alternative exits, hands heavy
with clubs.
    Eventually, following the disappearance
of dogs into subterranean darkness, the frightened
beasts would appear, eyes small and suspicious
in hard skulls.
    Blows would rain onto their backs,
reducing staunch vertebrae to the sponginess
of a discarded sofa, rib-bones like springs jutting
through the stiff hair of the coats.
    Not until
the sett had been completely unearthed, reduced to
a mere series of trenches, did the homecoming
occur, men quiet with tiredness and pride,
trudging matter-of-factly towards hearty breakfasts.

Stairs

Servants, but not servile, we're
an international brotherhood, dedicated
to the cause of social climbing. Lifts
have not supplanted us. They rise
and fall like guile machines; we represent
tradition, honest effort, the small spice

of a possible pratfall. Do not be deceived
by our identicalness. There is a hierarchy
even here; we all aspire to the landing,
few aware that our role is fixed.
The rules of the game require knowing
one's station, not getting uppity;

and if brogues smash us in the face
so be it. We have the compensation
of looking up skirts. Frequently hoovered,
we are afforded new leases of life.
Carpeting reduces the buffeting to an acceptable
degree. And existence is rarely boring:

there is usually much coming and going —
secretaries carrying files, bosses off
to a working lunch, young executives keen
on a midday game of squash, old ladies
who have to wait for their breath to catch
up with them. We go on for ever,

a Jacob's ladder to the stars.
Only occasionally, a block condemned,
will nemesis come — unexpectedly
chuntering through brick, a chained ball
slamming into immemorial identity.
Our luckier relatives get preservation orders.

The worst time is at night.
They leave a small light burning.
There is a nursery calm, but also
great hollowness. Echoes multiply.
No one needs us then. We feel forgotten.
We entertain terrifying dreams.

Sun Poem

Two white clouds handled
The greyness of dawn, breaking
Its shell. A sun slid,
Shining, out, its depth aching
With the pollen of brightness.
It fried in a second or less.

Then it was that flower,
That sunflower which lollops
About the garden wall hour
After hour, petals in dollops
Of radiance, quizzical look
As open as an open book.

Then it was the sun. Simply
Something sloughing simile
And metaphor, something hugely
Being not even the smile
Of morning; not an egg; not
A flower. Just gas. Round. Hot.

Tag

Hear the children's four-beat sonnet.
Watch them race around the yard —
"Watch out, Davy!" "Davy's on it."
Hit the wall, and hit it hard
For protection. Touch your neighbour.
Run like wind towards the trees!
See the fat boy puff and labour.
You evade his grasp with ease.
Sheila Saunders whizzes past me,
All her freckles thrown like dice.
"Girls are nice and boys are nasty!"
Sheila shouts, and skids like ice
From my clutches down the street,
And the poem is complete.

The Advent of Fatherhood

My wife is pregnant. I am thunderstruck.
 A swarm of responsibilities will come,
Low in the sky, that will be small, with luck,
 Bringing not much harm.

Within nine months our time will have run out
 As partners; it will have gatecrashed, un-
Invited and unplanned, yet not a lout,
 A sort of healthy cripple, needing someone

Constantly, until the illness of
 Littleness has shrunk and it has grown —
But all growth takes it from our warmth and love
 Until it stands alone.

The clichés lie in wait: photographs
 Of babyhood, bonnets, the law of wool,
That cherub face, those toothless liquid laughs,
 The smiling pot, the manikin at stool;

And then the faltering language, the daft lines
 So well intended,
The tottering, the falling flat, the whines
 And comforting, befriended

By the eternal mother in us all.
 I fear already measles, whooping cough,
The first-aid dash, the toy left in the hall
 On which I tread and instantly take off,

Thanks to its lethal wheels.
 I'm still a child inside; it thus seems mad
To consider soon how every father feels
 When first called Dad.

And what will it turn out like: applause
 Personified, or some squat, squirming dunce;
A saint or psychopath? Each killer was
 A baby once.

The Butt of all my Dreams

Sometimes you almost think there is no fault,
that he is Yin and I am Yang, and the two
of us are perfectly complementary. Two guys,
but two guys in harmony. But then you think,
lying awake solo in San Mateo at three
a.m., his strong back against your front,
that the Earth wants to come between you.
San Andreas sounds too much like some old moralist
from Rome, with all the power of God
at his elbow. The theory of isostasy states
that for every geological rise there is a corresponding
fall elsewhere, one part butch, the other sub-
dominant. When he prepares salad on the patio
at noon, I cannot believe it true. Just look
at those pectorals; no hammy old tragedian
with a crucifix, quoting Leviticus eighteen,
is going to gainsay that this is love. Plate
tectonics, hooey. But even now there are
rumblings: my hunger, then thunder over
Alameda and Santa Clara. What is
our yield point? Will we ever split? Are
the lithosphere and asthenosphere pertinent
to our discussion of who does the dishes,
who waters the flowers? I believe in fissures.
I believe in cracks and caves and cleavages.
But I also want to believe in a future.

The Girls at St Catherine's

What is it about the girls at St Catherine's:
Saintliness? No. Innocence? Ignorance means

The same thing at that age. To know is to be guilty of
Adulthood of a sort, to fall in love

Simply a commitment to the unprecedented
Experience. By soap scented

Rather than by perfume, by exercise rouged rather
Than by cosmetics, they stroll under a lather

Of cherry blossom. It is April in their lives.
Manhood hangs somewhere like a rack of knives.

  not starting from the top.
I hope you did not mind me
  rising to a stop.
So this is how you find me —

  feet, decanting woes.
that creep about on wary
  and mean as much as those
Words can be light and airy

  or sweep it from the room.
and symbol-ridden parlance,
  the poet's sense of doom
now and then can balance

  a little levity
unrelievedly serious;
  when poetry must be
I feel it's deleterious

  and hardly something worse.
eliciting a snigger
  out of a page of verse,
an unfamiliar figure

  a small attempt to cut
essentially it's harmless,
  and artificial, but
The project may seem charmless

On this what is your view?
a poem written backwards.
 rather than bend them to
One might be wise to lack words

 while passing on his bike.
a vicar pulling faces
 perverse, perhaps, and like
Starting from the base is

Turvy-Topsy

Twenty Minutes

We entered as another group were leaving.
Our black coats made us Russian politicians,
Sombre and snowbound; yet around us visions
Of summer blossomed. Everything was living.
We took our seats. The place did not feel sinister,
Merely sad. Untold scenes of grief
Had permeated everything. "His life
Should make us glad we knew him," said the minister
Chestily. A cheerless tape clicked on.
The curtains parted like the Red Sea waters,
Then joined again. Our father disappears
A million times towards the waiting oven.
We walked back to the cars and no one spoke.
The August sky had one thin skein of smoke.

Tyrell's Barn

Aladdin's Cave was great
But Tyrell's Barn was greater.
Beyond the five-bar gate
The yard stood, and beyond
The yard the banned
Barn, the alligator

Shed, the cayman isle.
Darkness stood at the door.
You never saw her smile.
Her secrets were her own.
Venturers turned to stone
Inside her, and the roar

Of silence deafened there.
Old Tyrell was long dead.
Mad he had been for sure.
His spirit stalked the place —
A disembodied face,
A rancid turnip head,

An ectoplasmic rustle
At which cats' ears bent back.
The paddock was all thistle.
The house was a bad shell.
Tyrell's Barn was whole,
However, from the crack

Of dawn to lingering dusks.
I never went inside.
The risks were all. The risks
Were visible as print.
It wore its evil scent
With unrepentant pride.

Unacknowledged Legislator

The poet has a poem accepted.
He tells his wife he is happy.
The cow jumped over the moon.
They are building motorway.
He gets twelve pounds.
Concorde refuels.

The poet has a poem rejected.
He tells his wife he is no longer happy.
Someone else gets twelve pounds.
The motorway inches forward.
Concorde farts thousands
in hot air.

The poet has another poem accepted.
He believes this makes two.
Twenty four pounds accumulates.
It is June already.
Thirteen American movies
have been started since January,

each with a budget beyond his wildest stanzas.
He updates daffodils.
Wordsworth did not have a patent on clouds
he thinks bravely.
He submits a poem hymning cumulonimbus.
It is promptly rejected.

Why? he asks. Why?
Do not the editor and I speak the same language?
Are we not kindred souls?
Did we not both take degrees
in English Literature?
It is August, and someone he has not met

tops the charts and starts a European tour.
Five thousand pounds a week
and all she had
was a CSE in domestic science.
Somebody in the City makes a killing.
The poet treads on a snail

on his way to the post-box.
Is this inauspicious? he wonders.
He deposits the envelope hesitantly.
He walks back avoiding the cracks
in the paving stones.
He daydreams about thirty six pounds.

Wanda at Dusk

*The last wolf native to Britain
was killed in 1743*

She professes to be steeped in ancient lore.
She has forsaken Swindon, and settled
near Clocaenog Forest in Clwyd.
Her circumstances are reduced, but her hair
burns auburn, and her eyes
are quartzite, hard and bright with the superiority
of secret knowledge. At nearby Cerrigydrudion
a fairy cow was milked into a sieve
by a witch until it went insane. Wanda
cites the Niska Indians of British Columbia
who in their totem ceremonies evoked
the wolf; and the beast-god of Lycopolis
in Egypt. She smiles. A cloud
scuds across the moon. It is the fifteenth
of February, Feast of Lupercalia.
She vaunts her power to protect the flocks
which graze these hillsides, or render them
vulnerable to stalking teeth, the hot breath
of mysterious slaughter. She interprets her name:
Teutonic for "wanderer". Soon she will
wander upon Hiraethog mountain where
the fairy cow was milked, there to perform
certain rites, pressed against
the sky, silhouetted upon the tufty grass,
as darkness cloaks the artificial waters
of the Alwen Reservoir.

Within a week, local press
and radio relate inexplicable carnage among
the Kerries and Cluns: throats ripped out, ribs
exposed, and everywhere the irrational print of wolf.

Writing to Alison Myers

At first it was easy. The goods had not arrived.
I dusted down my typewriter, yawned
as I reached for paper, frowned. Dear Ms . . . .
The goods would be on their way, Ms Myers claimed.
There was something about her phraseology
which I found affecting, like a hand on the shoulder
or a warm bedtime drink. It arrived, cracked.
I fumed, uncovering my typewriter. This time
Ms Myers would get an eyeful. Still the answer
came back reassuringly. I reconsidered. Yes,
perhaps I had been overly irate. I wrote,
apologizing. There was no reply. Summer
turned to autumn. The swallows fled,
like hatless Fred Astaires — just those coat tails,
to Africa. Leaves became self-consciously
pre-Raphaelite. I felt the autumnal equivalent
of sap in my veins. I unscrewed my fountain pen.
There were no complaints. I just wondered
how Miss Myers was getting on. She wrote back
noncommittally. Thank you for your letter.
Your goods should be arriving soon. If there
is any difficulty, please. . . . No, no, I wrote
in reply. Everything's fine. I simply needed
to know how you were. It's been a busy year.
The garden's looking good. Are you lonely too?
Alison Myers wrote back, the same dull print.
Thank you for your letter. We are sorry
that the goods were not in working order.
Please return them at your earliest convenience.
We hope we have not caused you undue bother.

ACKNOWLEDGEMENTS

Acknowledgements are due to *Acumen, Ambit, Anglo-Welsh Review, Argo, BBC Radio 3, Critical Quarterly, Encounter, Iron, Literary Review, London Magazine, New Statesman, Orbis, Other Poetry, Outposts Poetry Quarterly, Poetry Durham, Poetry Nottingham, Poetry Review, Poetry Wales, Quarto, South West Review, Thames Poetry, The Dalhousie Review, The Green Book, The Honest Ulsterman, The Listener, The Pen, The Times Literary Supplement, The Yeats Club Review, Tribune,* and *Wascana Review.*

'Hummingbird' appeared in Faber's *Poetry Introduction 3*

'Emma' and 'Unacknowledged Legislator' appeared in the Arvon Foundation's International Poetry Competition anthology